G.Poetry

by

Giselle Mendez

G. Poetry

CONTENTS:

In no particular order

Words about love, loss, pain,

growth, and forgiveness

DOOR TO MY HEART

Run,

With all of those

Insecurities you hold

With those trust issues

With those doubts that

True happiness exists

With your woes and worries

With your pain, tears, and

Lonely nights

Run...

But run straight towards

me

I'm ready

and here you are...

so quickly and effortlessly

you have made your way into my heart...

I've felt so far away from love for so long...

and here you are...

bringing me peace ...

bringing me comfort...

bringing back love...

oh, how far I've drifted from love...

and here you are...

bringing me back home.

My Dear

if only...

if only...

I can slow down time

to make our kisses last longer

my baby,

oh baby

how you've captured my entire heart...

now, let me...

just let me...

show you how

our 'forever' story

starts

As long as we're under the same moon...

I'll always feel close to you.

One day, my heart will stop asking for you.

One day, my dreams won't be about you

One day, my future plans won't include you.

Oh darling,

one day... when I speak about love,

you won't be the only thing on my mind.

One day, my days won't start

with thoughts of you on my mind.

One day, my nights won't end with wanting you.

One day, I promise one day...

just please not today.

How beautiful this language

sounding so foreign to my ear

but familiar to my heart...

every syllable,

every word,

every sentence.

Bound together to make up this language

of love that only my heart can translate.

Even after all of the
heartbreak

she endured in her past.

She left the light on

in her heart...

for me...

so I can find my way home...

I've met "the one" a few times in my life.

"the one" who showed me love unconditionally.

"the one" who broke my heart.

"the one" who had love for everyone but me.

"the one" who was patient with my process of rebuilding.

"the one" who made every excuse for why it couldn't be 'us.'

But what I've learned along the way is...

the most important "one" is

"the one" who stays and fights for

peace, love, and unity.

You're my "last one."

Darling.

I wrote pretty words

for your ugly heart

And

I'm sure you're

going crazy

And I'm sure you're in pain

But excuse me, if in this hurricane you created

I can't see your tears in the rain

We've known each other a while now

We were so different then

A darker version of our souls interacted with one
another

And now here we are,

Our souls a little brighter

Our smiles a little bigger

And our hearts a little fuller

Nice to meet you, again.

They say,

'the grass isn't always greener on the other side'

and I agree

But not this time

This time she was waiting for me

With a garden full of roses

In the skirts of green grass hills.

The picture you painted for us was vibrant

with colors I've never seen

The colors bled off of your paint brush,

there is the red for passion,

there is the yellow for our happiness,

and there is the blue for peace...

little did I know,

you were colorblind...

and in the end,

I would be the only one enjoying these colors

Enjoying our picture-perfect painting.

Alone.

Be patient with my heart

babe

For it walks towards love

A little wounded

When I was stuck in the rain

Stricken by heartbreak and pain

You took my shivering hand

And asked me to dance

She left you shattered

And I mended your broken

She sees you happy

Now a spark in her has awoken

She's come to claim you

As hers,

To sink her

Teeth deeper

Oh, silly girl, don't be naive

I found her

So now I keep her

How easy it was to love you

To be consumed by you

To devote my entire

Existence to bringing

happiness into your life

How easy it is to forget you

To strip my body from the

Scent of you

To devote my entire

existence to bringing

happiness into MY life

Are you patient
enough to

Rebuild me?

Selfless enough to love me?

Caring enough to heal me?

Smart enough to cherish me?

Didn't think so...

Move along baby

To love someone during

The 'good' times is easy

When the both of you are

in good places in your lives

but to love someone

through the 'hard' times

when their life is

breaking apart,

Now that's a fight not

Suitable for the weak

You doubted her

Pointed out her flaws

Punished her for her

Mistakes

Convinced her she was

Undeserving of love

Apologize to her

Look in that mirror

Beg her forgiveness

Love her

How naïve

To think your cold soul

Could warm my heart

May I,

Serenade your heart with

My sweet words

Trace your body with

My kiss

My touch

My tongue

How polite I shall be

with my introduction,

just to

disrespectfully

devour

every inch of you

oh, but if love could've

kept us together

we would've seen infinity

side by side

oh, darling

but we are built of more than

LOVE

Which is why we had to

Say

Goodbye

You took my hand

Then took my heart

Now everyday

You take my breath away

"but, how do you know it's real?"

she asked

"Because I'm not scared

to feel it,

I'm scared to lose it."

I'm glad I didn't find you sooner

I wasn't ready for you

Then

These wildfires remind me

Of you

The way you came into

My Life

And swept through

My heart

Mind

And soul

Then left me

With a cloud of dark

Smoke

Trying to breathe in life

again

Wish you would wrap

Yourself around me

The way your lips wrap

Around that bottle

But you choose to discover the depths of

The Henny

Rather than the depths of

me

there's a thin line

between my dreams and

nightmares

you're in one

and not the other

Guess?

I'm sorry

For allowing you to be

Collateral damage to this

Internal war I was

Facing

You deserved to have the

Best parts of me

Instead I gave you

Dreams with no reality

Beginnings with no end

Oh, that wicked tongue

How it danced so well in

Your pretty mouth

Left, right, up, down

How blessed your lips

Must have felt

When you would grace them

With your words

Oh, that wicked tongue

How it dances so well

Left, right, up, down

Building lie after lie

How unfortunate for your

Pretty mouth

I never believed in

'meant to be's'

or

'destiny'

Till my hand fit so

Perfectly in

Yours

She ate me in my entirety

She didn't dissect me

She didn't separate the

Parts of me that she

Didn't like

Everything that made me

Was

Everything that she

Needed

Everything that she

Desired

And I bet the sunrise was

Beautiful that morning

With shades of orange and

Reds across the sky

I'll never really know

How the sun rose or

How the sky glistened

That day

When, that morning...

As the sun rose and the

Shades of orange and red

Ran across the sky

It was HER I couldn't

Keep my eyes off of

I'll always wonder what

You were searching for at

The bottom of those

Bottles

Answers to your

Questions?

Yourself?

Pieces of me?

I guess I'll never know

Drink up, baby

I was so high on you

Overdosin'

These days I'm livin'

Sober

I'd be lying if I said

I didn't think of the

Relapse

One last time

To feel you in my veins

You look different these

Days

Change your hair?

Different shade of lipstick?

It's something...

Ahh, that smile

Haven't seen it in a while...

Happiness looks so good

On you

Even when it has nothing

To do with me

Your lips weren't always

Mine

Your hands weren't always

Mine

Your laugh

Your body

Your mind

Your soul

Your heart

I've come to terms with

The fact that you weren't

Always mine

But, now that you are

I have every intention to

Keep you 'mine'

forever

I know your past is dark

But I love you anyway

I know your smile at one point

Wasn't intended for me

But I love you anyway

I know when you planned your future

At one point, you didn't see me

But I love you anyway

We both made choices throughout our lives

That didn't include each other

But

Every decision

Every tear

Every laugh

Everything slowly designed us for each other

Perfectly

No matter what we go through

I'll love you anyway

I'll love you always

Even with all of the

Beautiful words

I can put together for you

"I love you"

will always be my favorite

How generous of you

To gift me all of these

Memories

Just before you left

I remember our first time

Yours; we were in the backseat

Of your car

You had a little too much to drink

And you were feeling brave

Mine; we were in my bed in Miami,

Sharing deep convo, laughs, and tears

And I was feeling brave

So beautiful

How I still remember our

First time saying

"I Love You"

to each other

The days are long

And the nights are even longer

The bed seems colder

And my body is the only

Thing that can keep you

Warm

Distance is our worst enemy

And the clocks run slower

Between the times we see

Each other

Be patient with me

Baby

I'm coming home soon

I've lived my life

Cautiously

Don't drive too fast

Don't swim after eating

Don't be out too late

Don't do this

Don't go there

Don't say that

Don't act this way or

That way

Exhausting...

Then I met you,

I dove head first into

Your heart

I removed the

'caution tape'

from my life

and for the first time

I felt like

Living dangerously

With you

You were

My highest of highs

And

My lowest of lows

My ultimate desire

And

My lethal addiction

You did a number on me

Wish you the best

And

Wish you the worst

There's no wrong way

To love someone

You love differently

You love the wrong ones

Yes...

But, love is love

Some aren't ready to receive

Some need more than others

Yes,

But, love is love

I never asked for all of

You

Just some of you

A small piece of your

Withered heart

To be dedicated to

Loving me

Those nightmares are

Keeping you up

What is it that torments

You in the night?

Low whimpers as you

Toss and turn

You're putting up a good

Fight

The daylight brings

Relief

Only a temporary high

Till darkness sets in

And there you go again

Battling those demons in the

night

I'd rather tattoo your name

On the inside

So

My heart can beat against it

And know that you're the reason

It has purpose again

Pride

What a funny thing

They say have pride in

who you are

And what you do

Pride shows confidence and assertiveness

They also say,

In a relationship

Pride will cause prolonged

Arguments, anger, and frustration

So be proud

But

Don't be prideful

Tell me

What has made you cold?

You shiver in the summer

And find comfort in the winter

Tell me your story

Come sit by my fire

Fight for love

Fighting to stay in love

Fight to have you love me more

Fighting to love you more

Fought so much while we

Were in love

Fought to hold on to what love

We had left

Fought for you

Fought with you

Fought with myself

Fought for us

Fight for love

Fighting to stay in love

Distance: an amount of

space between two things

or people

You fear the distance

will make me distant

that different times zones

will postpone our milestones

that somehow time apart

will change what's in my heart

2,687 miles from you

2,687 miles from me

Distance:

Only makes me

Miss you more

Want you more

Love you more

You implored consistency

Not too much to ask for

I guess...

After all,

You've master it

Consistently,

Uncommunicative

Inconsiderate

Unapologetic

Unavailable

Unreliable

Distracted

Apathetic

Secretive

I asked for consistency

As well,

But for traits you

Could not generate

Kind of beautiful, isn't it?

How

A song

A location

A movie

Anything can trigger

Memories of someone

Good memories

Sad memories

Memories so deeply buried

You almost forgot they happened

To live in the moment is nice

But, to be remembered

Over and over again...

Now, that's kind of beautiful,

Isn't it?

And I loved you

And you loved me

Then I loved her

And you loved me

Then I loved you

And you loved her

Now I love her

And you love her

And you and I...

Strangers

Tell me about her

Her likes and dislikes

Her passions and troubles

I want to know her the

Way that I know you

Because if

You're mine

Then

She's mine

I was only protecting my

heart

It had been broken before

I was only making sure

They would stay

Not many ever did

I was only trying not to

Be vulnerable

People take advantage

In protecting and guarding myself

I forgot to love...

I forgot to allow myself

To be loved

Beautiful distraction

Meant to distract me

How can I resist

When you insist

Tormenting temptation

Oh, how you have tempted me

Captivating eyes

Release me from your

Captivity

I found you today

Not in a photo or

In person

I found you in the

burrows of my memory

Could've been a scent

Or a song that triggered

But there you were

Laughing

Smiling

Dancing

Did I make you laugh?

Were you just being your goofy self?

Dance away...

Thank you for this...

This memory of you

When we had you close

Nice to see you again...

Until next time

Fade into me

Till we become one

Till we can't tell where

You start and I finish

Fade into me

Run through my veins

And settle in my chest

Let me breathe you in

Let me feel you in me

Pretty sure that's how

Our souls become one...

Hello, Soulmate

Does it reach out for me?

While you dream?

Has your body accepted

That it'll no longer feel

My warmth next to you?

Or is it going through withdrawals?

Yearning for me

I don't blame it...

What we had was always a

Little bit of an

Addiction

Moments of a better time

When I was a better version

Of me

And you were a better

Version of you

Promises of forever

Spoken into the universe

Maybe,

The universe took a day off

Maybe,

The universe missed our call while

attending to others

Or maybe, just maybe...

The universe responded

But we didn't care for

the answer

because we still promised each other forever

when the universe could

only give us moments

Beautiful moments

What secrets do these

Four walls hold?

Is that why they creak in

The night?

Hoping for someone to

Listen

What secrets are they

Holding for you?

What have they seen and

Heard?

Let these walls cave in

Let us hear their secrets

After all,

What do you have to hide?

We all have our demons

Some just live with them better

Than others

I drink to remember you

Sober, I shut you out

But,

with the day I had

and,

a night like this

I steady sip

Rush in

These next few hours...

My mind is yours

Was I too nice?

Too passive

Too considerate

Too affectionate

Too understanding

Too clingy

Too needy

Too jealous

Tell me...

Because as I was focused

On all of the reasons

Why we were so perfect for

Each other

You were looking for the

Reasons we were not

Forever: for all future time; for always

Seems like we had our own definition of

'forever'

Mine,

Allowed me to forgive

To communicate

To understand

To cherish and

Love unconditionally

Yours,

didn't

To be loved by you

What a beautiful thing

To be loved by you

My partner

My confidant

My best friend

Oh,

To be loved by you

How beautiful

But to love you

To be in love with you...

How lucky am I.

Without your

"Good Morning" text

I will have one anyway

Without you calling me

"Beautiful"

I will continue to be

Without your hopes for

"Sweet Dreams"

I will have them anyway

You see,

You added to my life

But have no right to subtract

Don't worry your little heart

My thoughts are yours

My laughs are yours

My moans are yours

My body is yours

My heart is yours

My soul calls out for only you

Don't worry your little heart

I'm all yours

Yes,

I could've kept fighting for you

Fighting for your love

Till my knuckles bled

But the funny thing about

A fight is...

Only one person wins in the

end

I didn't need you to save me

I could do that all by myself

I just needed you to stay

But staying required effort

And of course

That's too much to ask from you

Poor you

Always wanting for someone to

Invite you in

But never willing to stay

You didn't sign up to be my hero

To save me from all the things that

Bring me torment

And yet,

Here you are

With a spear in hand

And a shield in the other.

Today I needed you

I fought myself to call you

To reach out to you

You said you would be there

Always

Pinky promised

So why do I hesitate?

Maybe,

I was never good at speaking up

or

You were never good at keeping promises

I craved adventure

So, I took myself places

I've never been

I craved you

Because you took my heart

Places it's never been

I shut the door

And

You find a window

Oh, my love,

How you try and save me from

Myself

I keep it dark in here,

You bring in the light

Save me?

You just might

You told me

1000 times you loved me

and

1000 times I melted

1000 times our hearts synced

and

1000 times I was "the one"

1000 times I believed you

and

1000 times I forgave you

for those

1000 times you gave me

1000 hopes that we would live and love for

1000 years

I didn't need 1000 of anything

Just one that was true

The world can forget me

But not you...

I'm burrowed in your chest

I sing to your heart

And dance around between heartbeats

I dreamt of you

Spoke you into the universe

Every 11:11, you were my only wish

Every breath onto my candles

Carried only your name

I dare you to feed me to the

Wolves of your soul

I will hunt with them side by side

I will learn their ways

And together

We will devour your demons

I'll be their Alpha

And your heart

Will be my moon

HEAR ME HOWL

They can keep their ordinary love

Because what we have

Is everything but

We swim in the skies

and

Fly in the oceans

Float on the sands of the desert

And

Dive deep into the shallows

Us?

Ordinary?

Oh baby,

We are everything but

Oh, this white-knuckle love

Gripping the pieces of you

That are left

Bloody knees won't make you stay

And

This white-knuckle love

Won't keep you from fading away.

All of the signs

pointed to you

They were

STOP

signs

But I ran through them anyway

The lights flashed yellow

To at least slow down

But when it came to you

It was always

Full throttle

I didn't need healing

But you brought the bandages anyway

Where have you been girl?

Who taught you to always be prepared to

Heal your partner?

So much to carry

But you do it with a smile

No more healing.

Let's just grow.

I'll wait

Even when you didn't ask me to

How could I not?

When you came

And shook my entire life around

How could I go back to

anything less than you?

So now I wait...

With no definitive ending

Easy to love you when

The lights are low

Not my idea of taking it slow

In this room, your body meets mine

You're an open book after a bottle of wine.

Let me flip through your pages

Let me fall for you word by word.

They say "guilt" will eat you alive

But not you

You sat at the table with "guilt"

Invited "guilt" into your bed

Night after night

You committed to "guilt" more than you ever committed to anyone

Does "guilt" keep you warm on

Those lonely nights?

Does "guilt" heal your

Self-inflicted wounds?

Does "guilt" know you call me?

Do you both call me side by side?

Does "guilt" encourage these words of

"I'm sorry"   and   "I miss you"

between sobs?

I hope you live happily ever after

You and "guilt"

Deserve each other

I stopped drinking

Because you intoxicated every

Part of me

I stopped smoking

Because loving you has left me

Just as high

Paint me

With all of those colorful words

You used to describe me

Some days

"crazy"

some days

"baby"

Oh, what a masterpiece it shall be.

The moment of truth

Was the scariest place to be

There you were

In your most vulnerable state

And there I was

Ready to take it all in

"I forgive you"

She said

As she balled her fist in the pockets

Of her sweater

Her eyes glazed with tears

"I forgive you"

she said again

As if this time she was trying to convince herself

Of these words

She had to forgive her

Hate would only suffocate her

And

Silence would leave her empty

You borrowed my heart

Almost like stole

My heart

But with every intention of

Giving it back

Where to find giselle Mendez

INSTAGRAM: g.poetry00

g.poetry00@gmail.com